BOUNDLESS BOOKS

...ristmas Carol, Charles Dickens • The Scarlet Letter, Nathaniel Hawthorne • Bartleby, the Scrivener, Herman Melville • Cranford, Elizabeth Gaskell • The Warden, Anthony Trollope • Silas Marner, George Eliot • Fathers and Sons, Ivan T... ...ce's Adventures in Wonderland, Lewis Carroll • Thérèse Raquin, Émile Zola • Around the World in Eighty Days, Jules Verne • Eight Cousins, or the Aunt-Hill, Louisa May Alcott • The Adventures of Tom Sawyer, Mark Twain • A Doll... ...rik Ibsen • Flatland, Edwin Abbott Abbott • The Strange Case of Dr. Jekyll and Mr. Hyde, Robert Louis Stevenson • A Study in Scarlet, Arthur Conan Doyle • The Jungle Book, Rudyard Kipling • The Importance of Being Earnest, Oscar... ...ano de Bergerac, Edmond Rostand • The Reluctant Dragon, Kenneth Grahame • The Turn of the Screw, Henry James • The War of the Worlds, H. G. Wells • Heart of Darkness, Joseph Conrad • The Awakening, Kate Chopin • The Wonderf... ...L. Frank Baum • White Fang, Jack London • Ethan Frome, Edith Wharton • Peter Pan, J. M. Barrie • The Celestial Omnibus and Other Stories, E. M. Forster • O Pioneers!, Willa Cather • The Dead, James Joyce • The Metamorphosis, Franz... ...Man Jeeves, P. G. Wodehouse • The Mysterious Affair at Styles, Agatha Christie • Crome Yellow, Aldous Huxley • Siddhartha, Hermann Hesse • The Curious Case of Benjamin Button, F. Scott Fitzgerald • "The Shunned House," H. P. Lo... ...op's Fables, Aesop • The Oedipus Plays, Sophocles • Beowulf, Anonymous • Utopia, Thomas More • A Midsummer Night's Dream, William Shakespeare • Candide, Voltaire • The Castle of Otranto, Horace Walpole • The Sorrows of Young... ...ann Wolfgang von Goethe • Grimm's Fairy Tales, Brothers Grimm • Frankenstein; or, The Modern Prometheus, Mary Wollstonecraft Shelley • "The Legend of Sleepy Hollow," Washington Irving • The Girl with the Golden Eyes, Honoré de...

BOUNDLESS BOOKS

50 LITERARY CLASSICS
TRANSFORMED INTO WORKS *of* ART

By Postertext

CHRONICLE BOOKS

SAN FRANCISCO

To my grandmother

BOUNDLESS BOOKS LIST OF TRANSLATORS:

Page 8, Aesop's Fables, by Aesop, translation by George F. Townsend
Page 10, The Oedipus Plays, by Sophocles, translation by F. Storr
Page 13, *Beowulf*, by Anonymous, translation by Francis B. Gummere
Page 16, *Utopia*, by Thomas More, translation by Gilbert Burnet
Page 18, *Candide*, by Voltaire, translation by William F. Fleming
Page 23, *The Sorrows of Young Werther*, by Johann Wolfgang von Goethe, translation
by R. D. Boylan
Page 28, *Grimm's Fairy Tales*, by Brothers Grimm, translation by Edgar Taylor
and Marian Edwardes
Page 34, *The Girl with the Golden Eyes*, by Honoré de Balzac, translation by
Ellen Marriage
Page 51, *Fathers and Sons*, by Ivan Turgenev, translation by Constance C. Garnett
Page 58, *Thérèse Raquin*, by Émile Zola, translation by Edward Vizetelly
Page 59, *Around the World in Eighty Days*, by Jules Verne, translation by George
Makepeace Towle
Page 68, *A Doll's House*, by Henrik Ibsen, translation by Unknown
Page 80, *Cyrano de Bergerac*, by Edmond Rostand, translation by Gladys Thomas
and Mary F. Guillemard
Page 112, *The Metamorphosis*, by Franz Kafka, translation by David Wyllie
Page 123, *Siddhartha*, by Hermann Hesse, translation by Gunther Olesch, Anke
Dreher, Amy Coulter, Stefan Langer, and Semyon Chaichenets

Library of Congress Cataloging-in-Publication Data:
Names: Postertext Pte. Ltd., artist.
Title: Boundless books : 50 literary classics transformed into
   works of art / By Postertext.
Description: San Francisco : Chronicle Books, 2016.
Identifiers: LCCN 2015044786 | ISBN 9781452148649 (alk. paper)
Subjects: LCSH: Book design—Miscellanea. | Books and reading in art. | Words
   in art.
Classification: LCC Z246 .P67 2016 | DDC 686—dc23 LC record available at
http://lccn.loc.gov/2015044786

Manufactured in China

Designed by Kristen Hewitt

Chronicle Books publishes distinctive books and gifts.
From award-winning children's titles, bestselling cookbooks,
and eclectic pop culture to acclaimed works of art and design,
stationery, and journals, we craft publishing that's instantly
recognizable for its spirit and creativity. Enjoy our publishing
and become part of our community at www.chroniclebooks.com.

10 9 8 7 6 5 4 3 2 1

Chronicle Books LLC
680 Second Street
San Francisco, CA 94107
www.chroniclebooks.com

CONTENTS

INTRODUCTION

A picture is worth a thousand words.

We take this adage literally. At Postertext, every piece of art we make captures the spirit of a classic book in a way that would make its author proud. To achieve this often elusive goal, we read the entire book from cover to cover before attempting any brainstorming or illustrative work. Only after everyone involved in the project understands the plot, motifs, moods, symbols, and themes do we start our design process. We work with a team of talented artists and book experts from all over the world to ensure that our art prints are visually stunning and true to each book.

Creating visuals to represent a novel is no easy task. The designs you see here are the results of countless hours of research and discussions. Every person interprets a story differently, which is why reading fiction involves an act of creativity—with your mind transforming words on the page into pictures that come alive in your head. Our job is to capture those delightful pictures and illustrate them alongside the text. It is always a challenging task, and the project of making a book out of our art prints seemed at first even more of a challenge, even an impossible task: Fit entire works of literature that normally take up entire books or large canvases into just one or two pages. In addition, each art print needs to end flush with the last corner of the page, meaning that despite the massively varying lengths of text, every novel ends exactly where the illustration ends, and with close-to-identical font sizes.

This book contains a collection of illustrations made entirely out of text from fifty select classics. It is the perfect companion for any book lover who appreciates art and design. Read timeless classics from up close, or stand back and watch the words coalesce into elegant illustrations. Each page or spread contains the entire text of the book, and the text is legible without any reading aids—but a magnifying glass is included to help with the reading. Turn the pages to read the classics in a new way.

Aesop's Fables

Aesop

c. 620–560 BCE

The Oedipus Plays:
Oedipus the King and *Oedipus at Colonus*

Sophocles
c. 430 BCE (*Oedipus the King*) and
c. 401 BCE (*Oedipus at Colonus*)

Beowulf

Anonymous

c. 700–1000

Utopia

Thomas More
1516

☞

A Midsummer Night's Dream

William Shakespeare
1590–1597

Candide

Voltaire

1759

The Castle of Otranto

Horace Walpole
1764

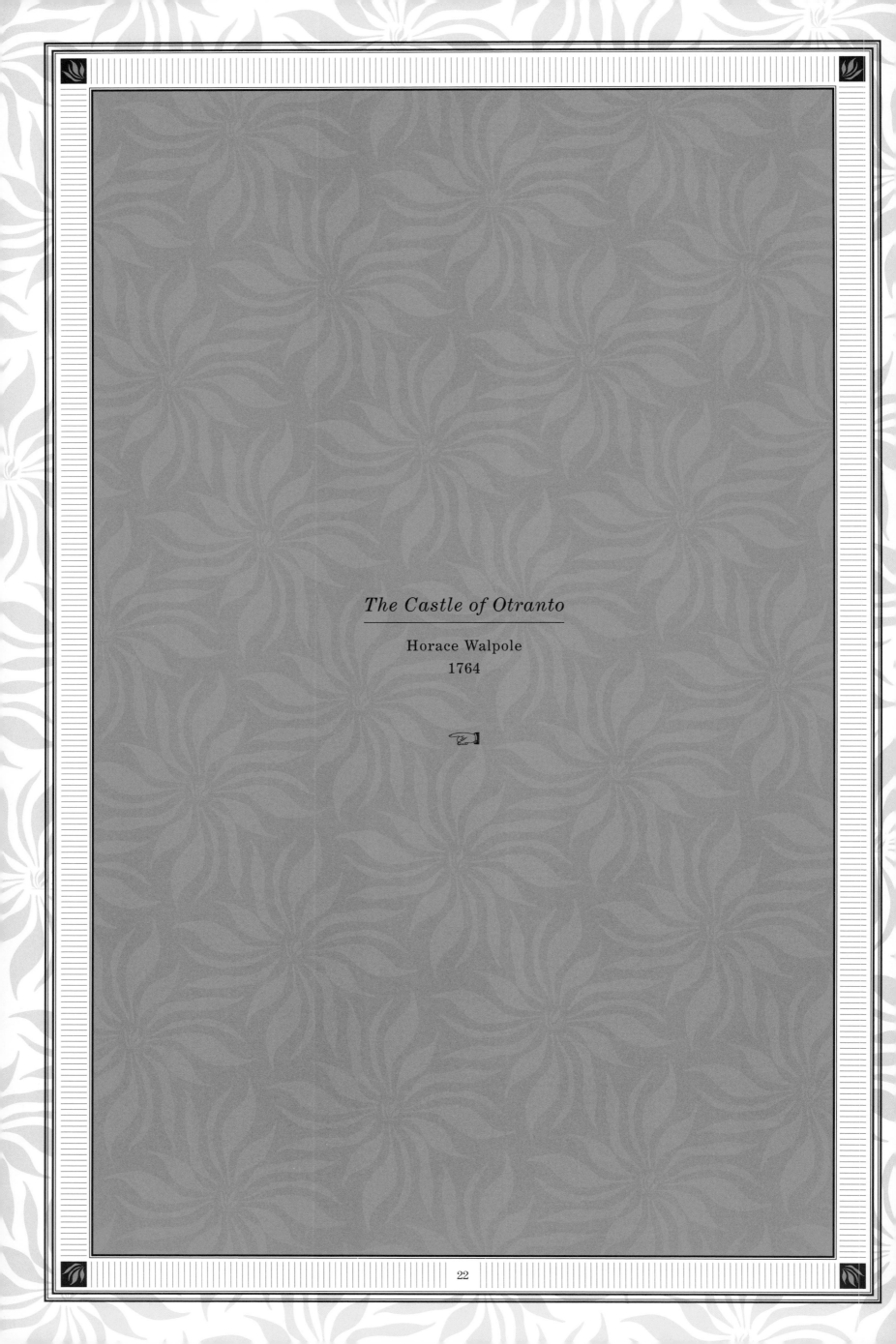

The Sorrows of Young Werther

Johann Wolfgang von Goethe
1774

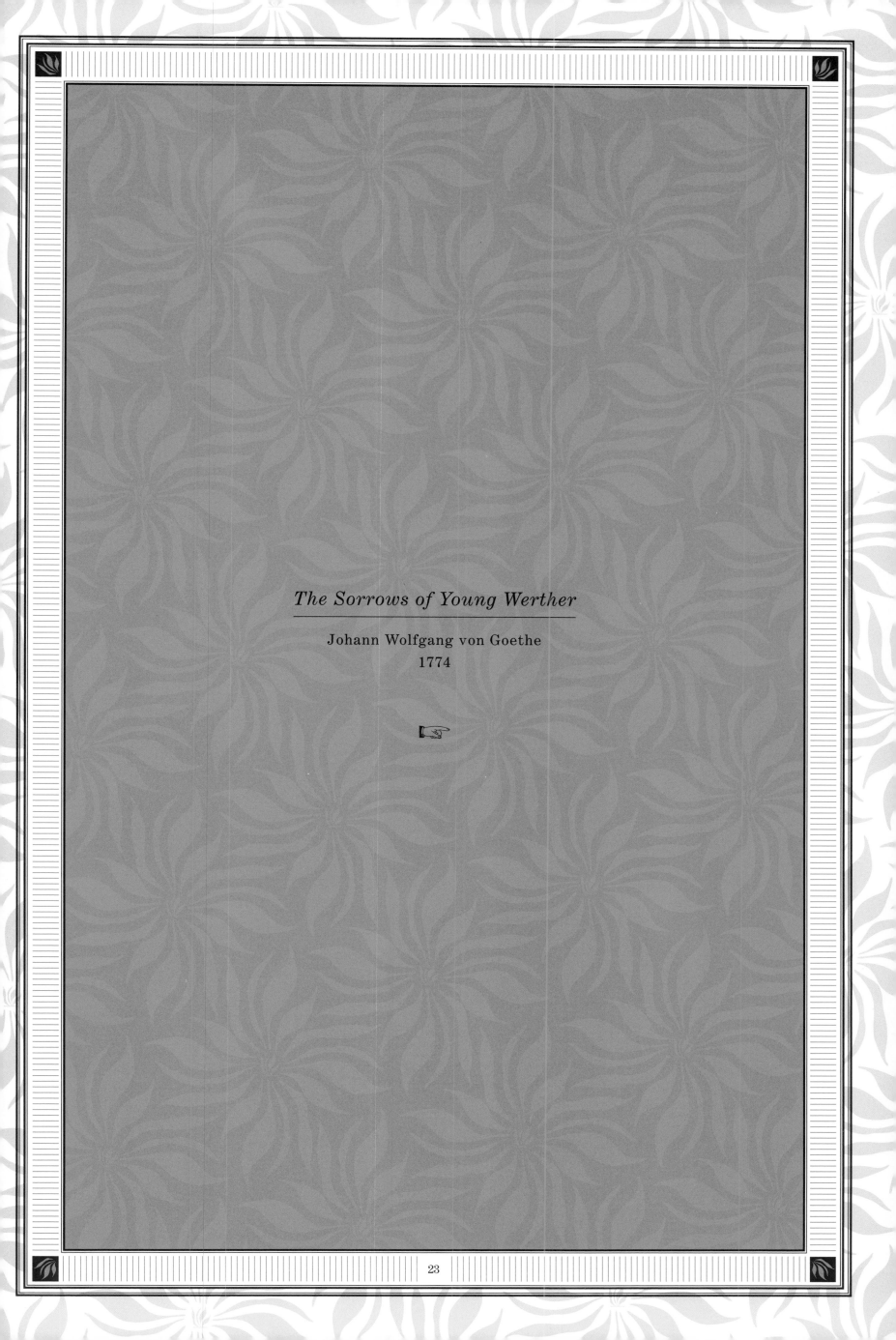

Grimm's Fairy Tales: Various stories*

Brothers Grimm
1812

* "The Golden Bird," "Hans in Luck," "Jorinda and Jorindel," "The Travelling Musicians," "Old Sultan," "The Straw, the Coal and the Bean," "Briar Rose," "The Dog and the Sparrow," "The Twelve Dancing Princesses," "The Fisherman and His Wife," "The Willow-Wren and the Bear," "The Frog-Prince," "Cat and Mouse in Partnership," "The Goose-Girl," "The Adventures of Chanticleer and Partlet," "Rapunzel," "Fundevogel," "The Valiant Little Tailor," "Hansel and Gretel," "The Mouse, the Bird, and the Sausage," "Mother Holle," "Little Red-Cap [Little Red Riding Hood]," "The Robber Bridegroom," "Tom Thumb," "Rumpelstiltskin," "Clever Gretel," "The Old Man and His Grandson," "The Little Peasant," "Frederick and Catherine," "Sweetheart Roland," "Snowdrop," "The Pink," "Clever Elsie," "The Miser in the Bush," "Ashputtel," "The White Snake," "The Wolf and the Seven Little Kids," "The Queen Bee," "The Elves and the Shoemaker," "The Juniper-Tree," "The Turnip," "Clever Hans," "The Three Languages," "The Fox and the Cat," "The Four Clever Brothers," "Lily and the Lion," "The Fox and the Horse," and "The Blue Light"

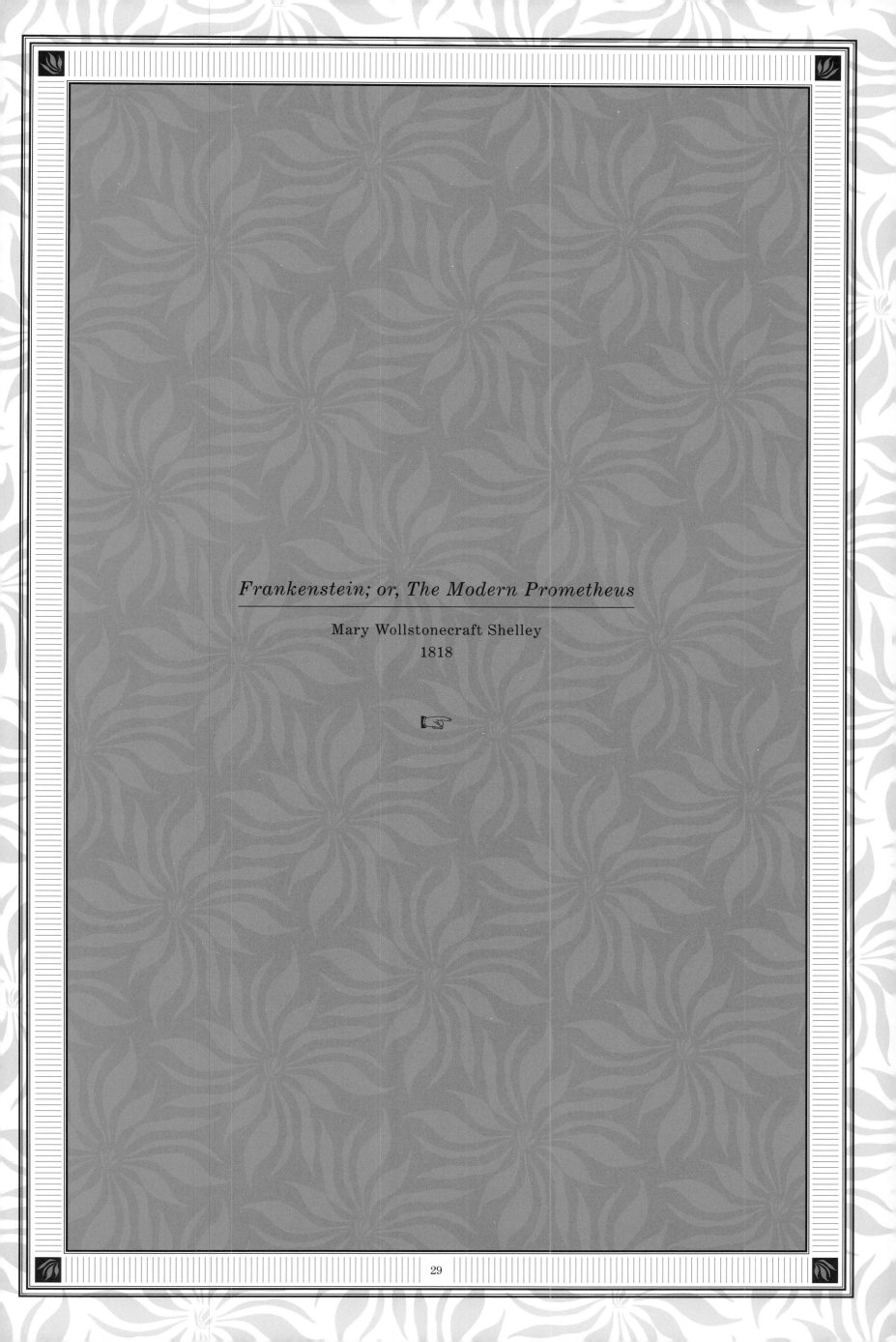

Frankenstein; or, The Modern Prometheus

Mary Wollstonecraft Shelley
1818

"The Legend of Sleepy Hollow"

Washington Irving
1820

The Girl with the Golden Eyes

Honoré de Balzac

1835

A Christmas Carol

Charles Dickens
1843

The Scarlet Letter

Nathaniel Hawthorne
1850

☞

Bartleby, the Scrivener

Herman Melville
1853

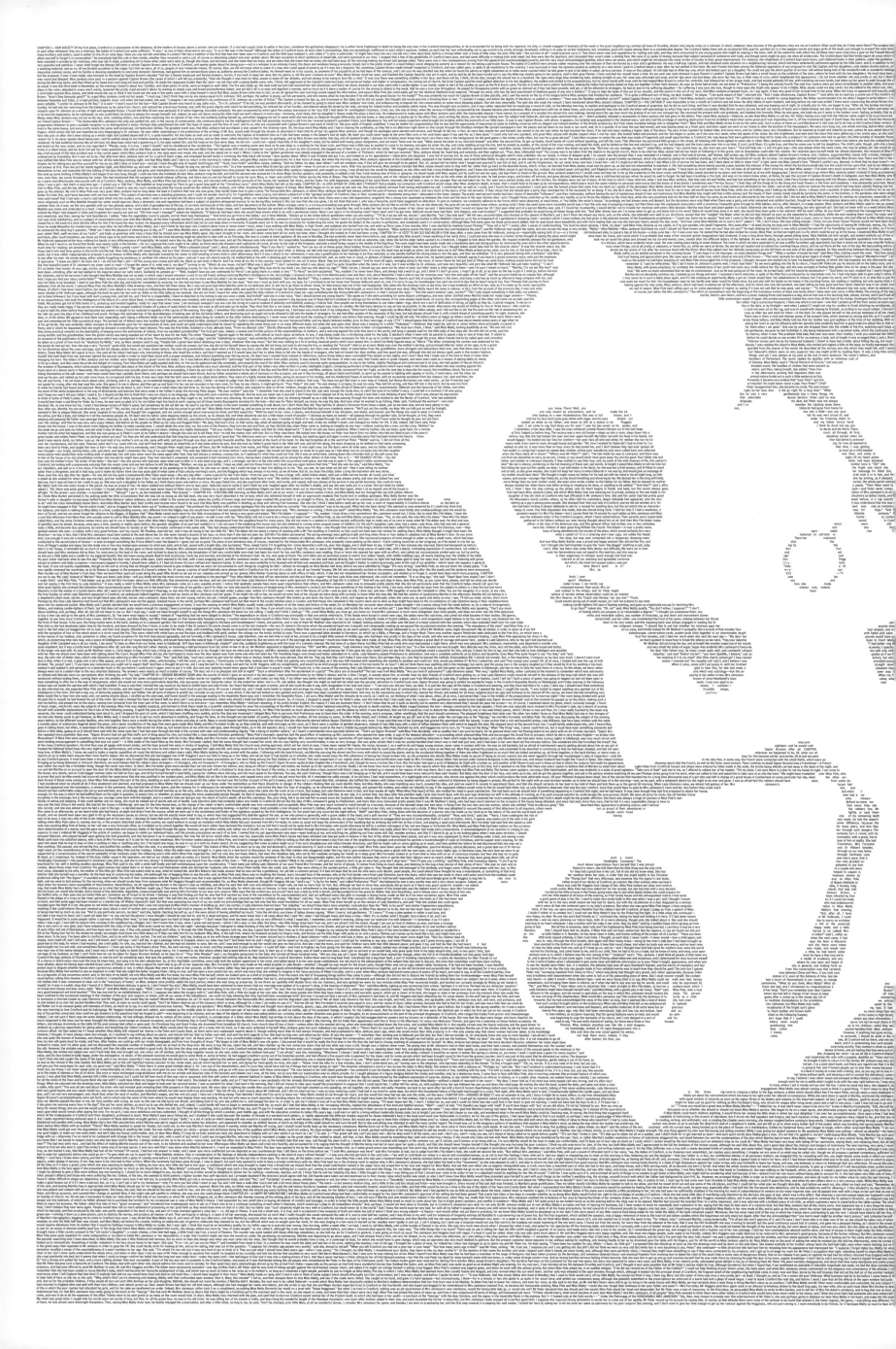

Cranford

Elizabeth Gaskell
1853

The Warden

Anthony Trollope
1855

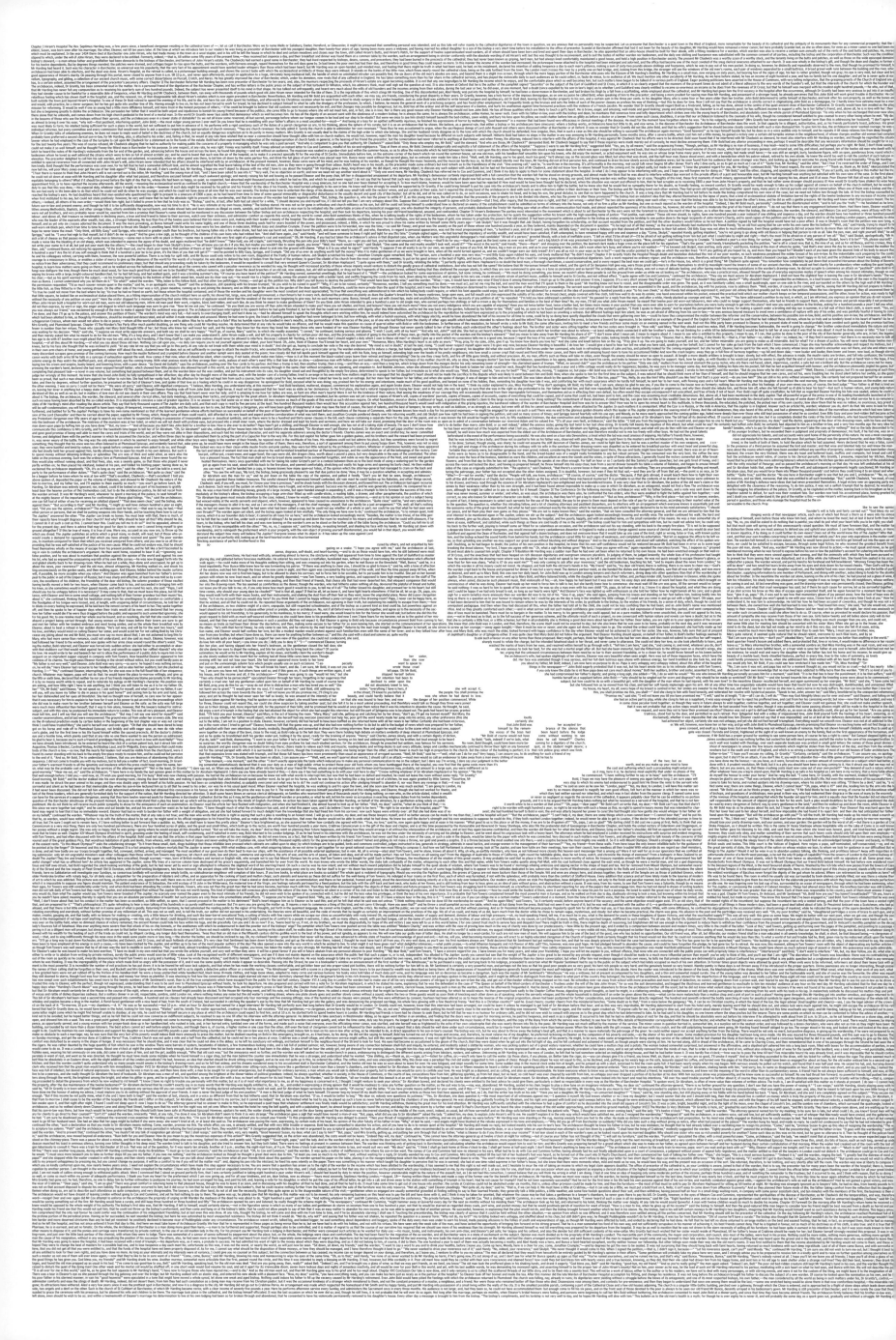

PART ONE CHAPTER 1

In the days when the spinning-wheels hummed busily in the farmhouses—and even great ladies, clothed in silk and thread-lace, had their toy spinning-wheels of polished oak—there might be seen in districts far away among the lanes, or deep in the bosom of the hills, certain pallid undersized men, who, by the side of the brawny country-folk, looked like the remnants of a disinherited race.

Silas Marner

George Eliot
1861

Fathers and Sons

Ivan Turgenev
1862

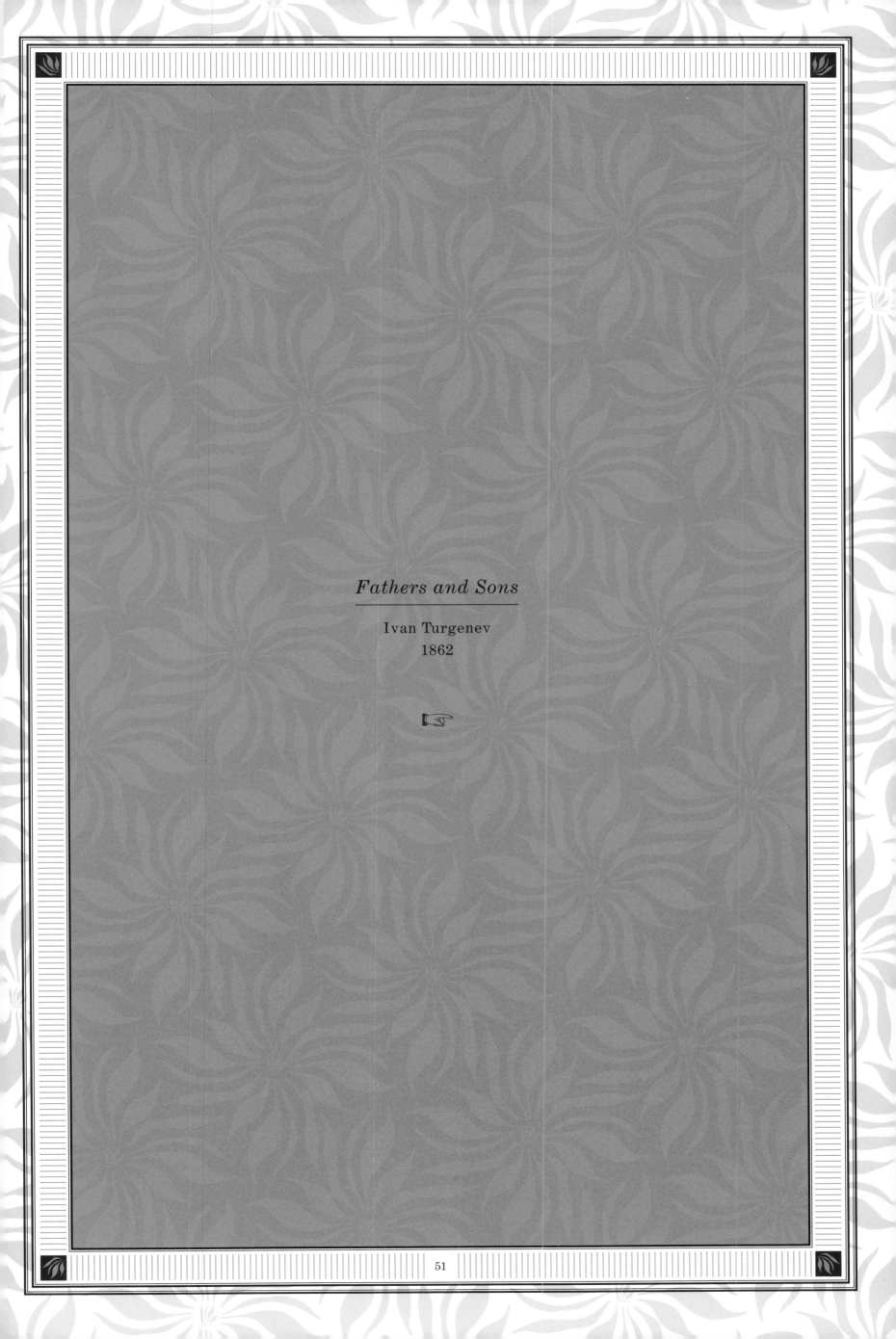

Alice's Adventures in Wonderland

Lewis Carroll

1865

Thérèse Raquin

Émile Zola
1867

Around the World in Eighty Days

Jules Verne
1873

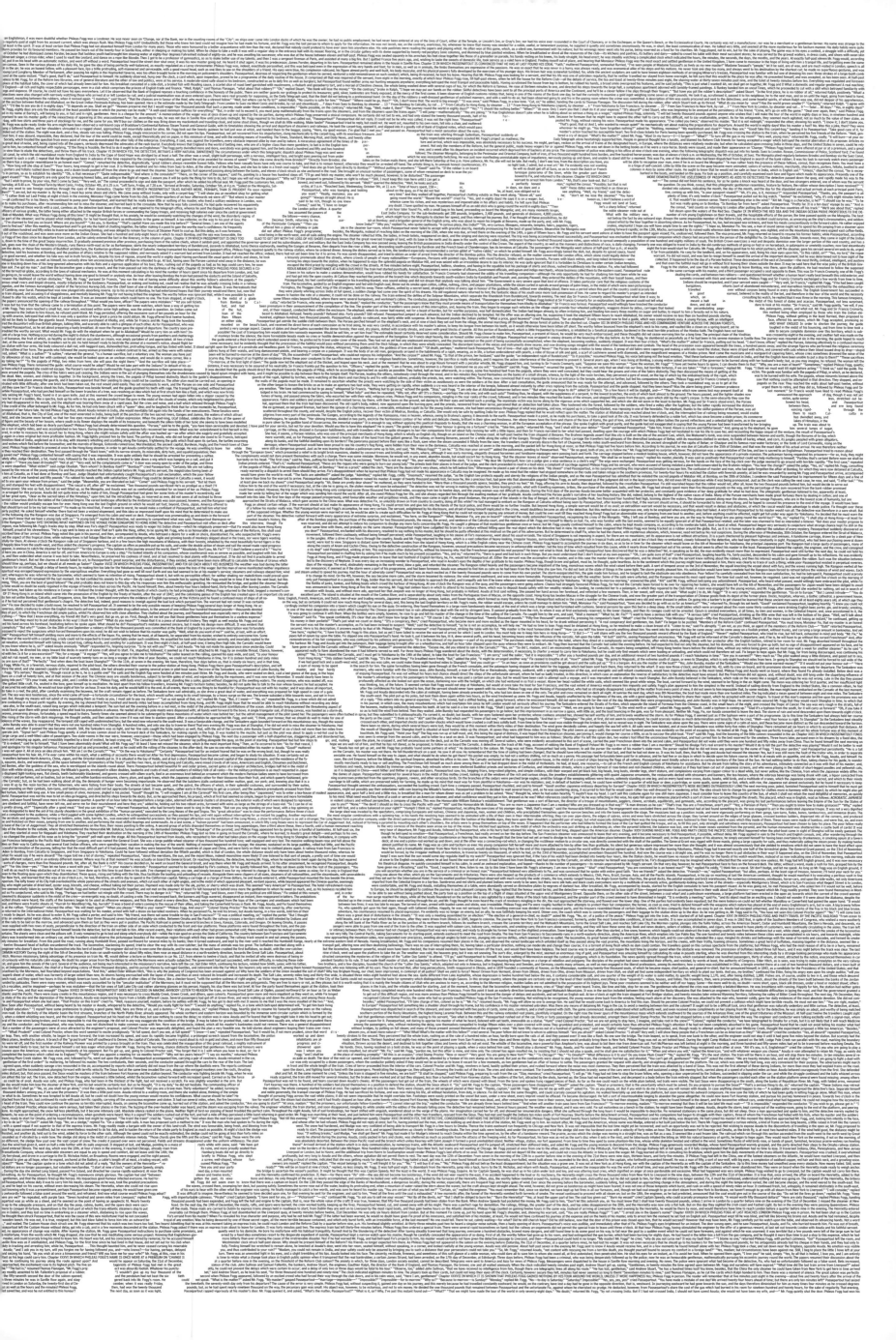

Eight Cousins, or the Aunt-Hill

Louisa May Alcott
1875

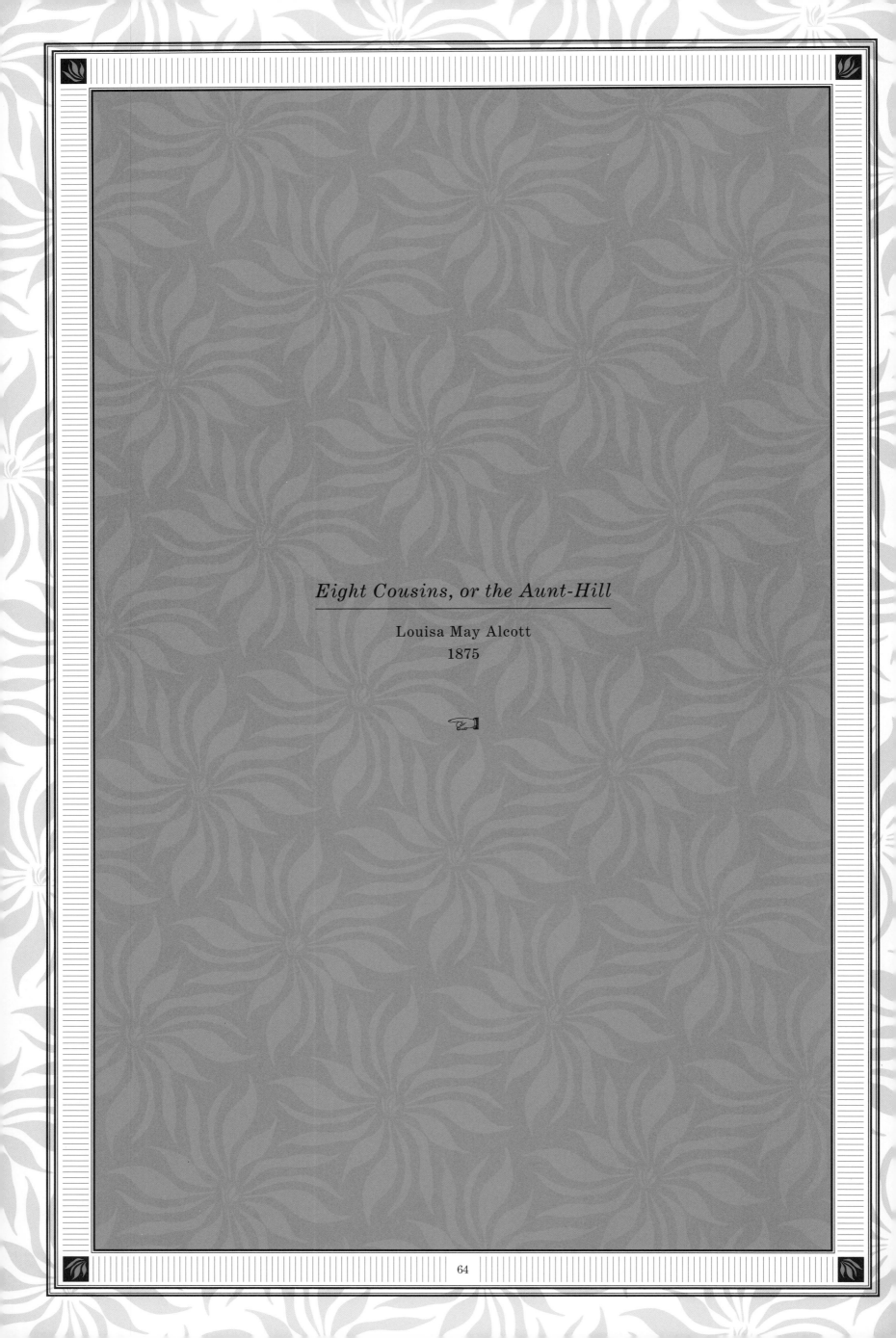

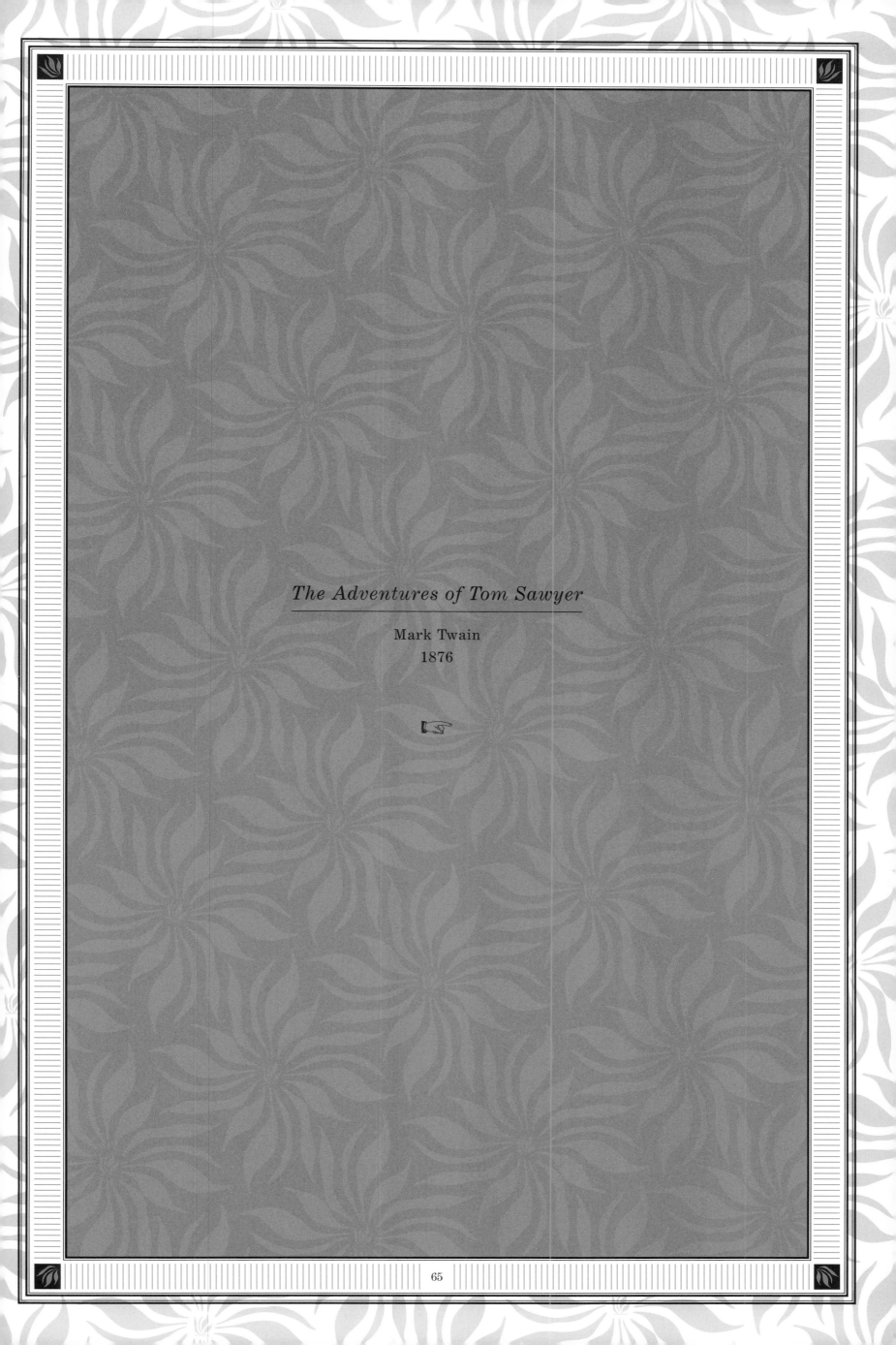

The Adventures of Tom Sawyer

Mark Twain
1876

A Doll's House

Henrik Ibsen
1879

Flatland

Edwin Abbott Abbott

1884

The Strange Case of Dr. Jekyll and Mr. Hyde

Robert Louis Stevenson
1886

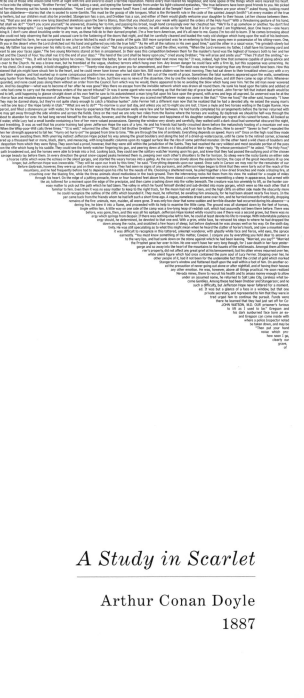

A Study in Scarlet

Arthur Conan Doyle

1887

The Jungle Book

Rudyard Kipling

1894

The Importance of Being Earnest

Oscar Wilde

1895

Cyrano de Bergerac

Edmond Rostand

1897

The Reluctant Dragon

Kenneth Grahame
1898

The Turn of the Screw

Henry James
1898

The War of the Worlds

H. G. Wells
1898

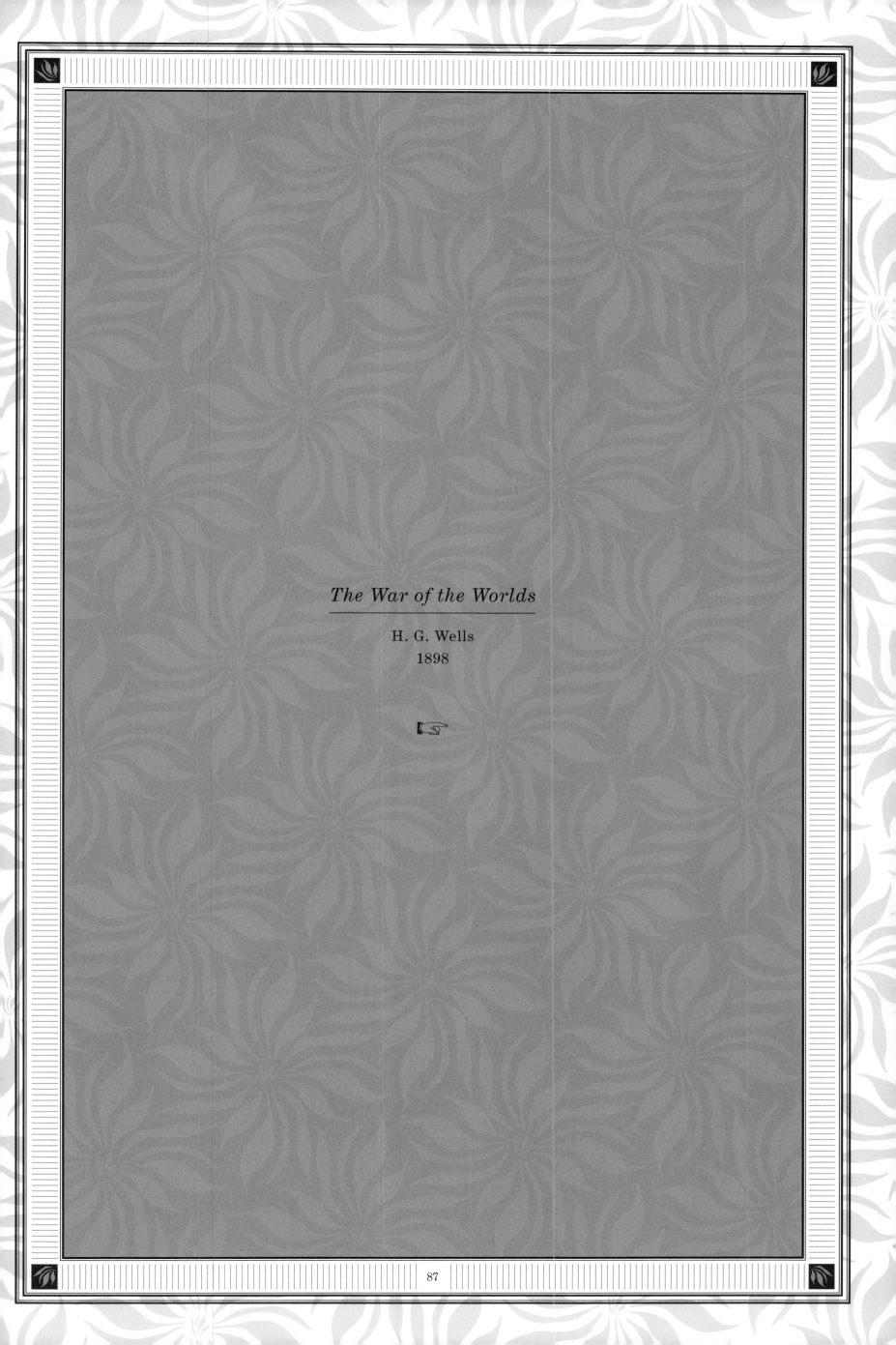

Heart of Darkness

Joseph Conrad

1899

The Awakening

Kate Chopin
1899

The Wonderful Wizard of Oz

L. Frank Baum
1900

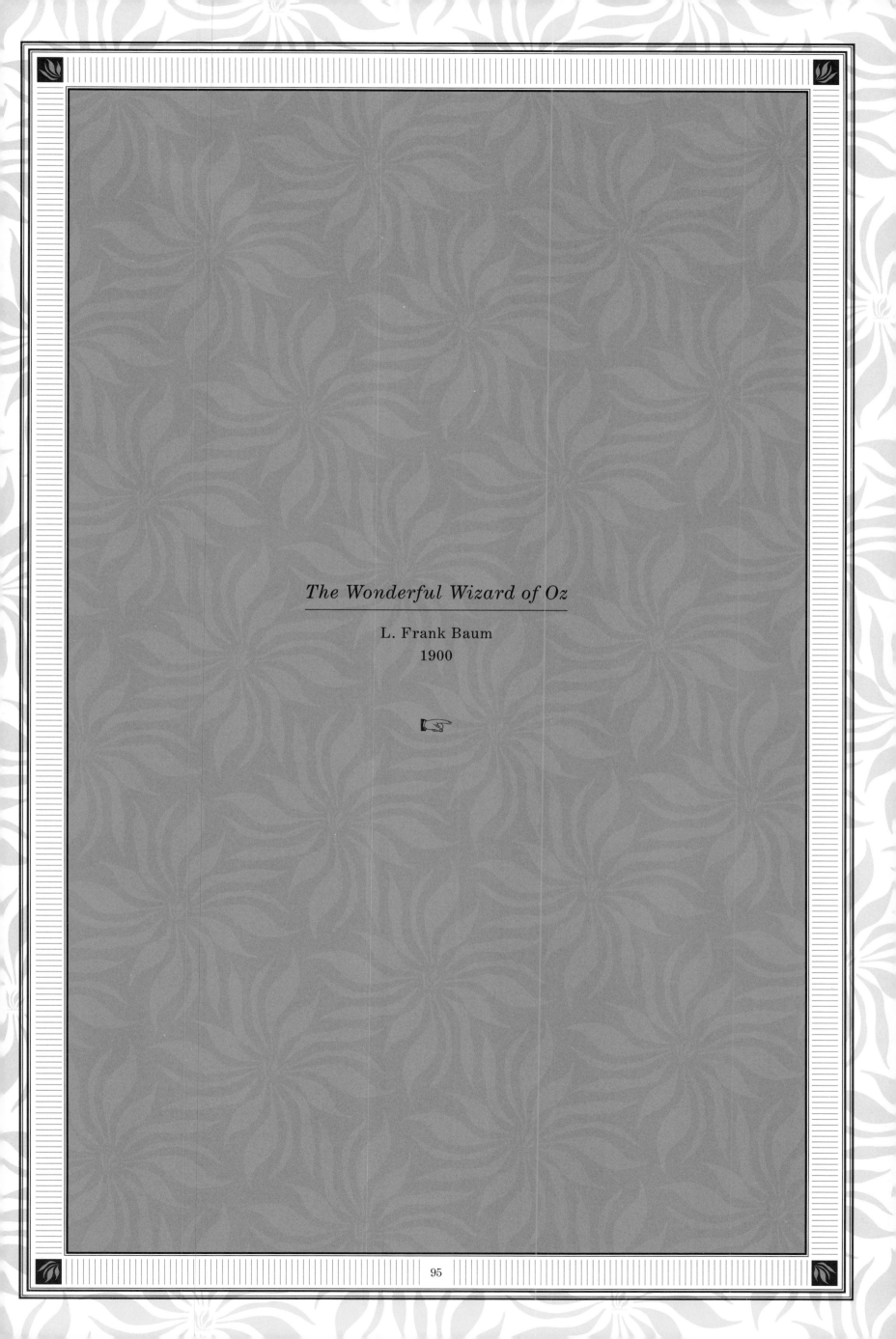

White Fang

Jack London
1906

Ethan Frome

Edith Wharton
1911

Peter Pan

J. M. Barrie

1911

The Celestial Omnibus and Other Stories:
"The Celestial Omnibus" and "The Road from Colonus"

E. M. Forster
1911

O Pioneers!

Willa Cather
1913

The Dead

James Joyce
1914

110

The Metamorphosis

Franz Kafka
1915

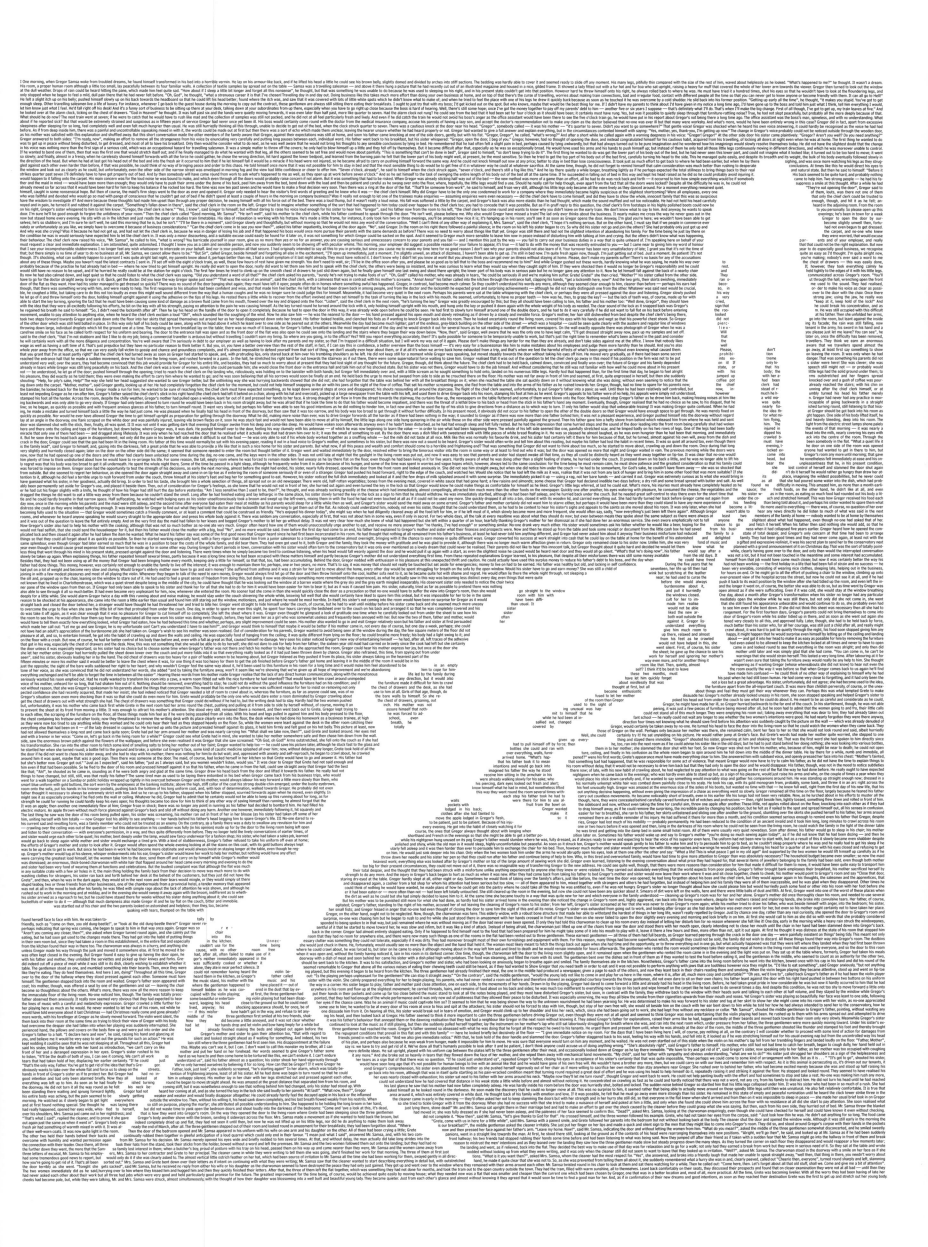

My Man Jeeves

P. G. Wodehouse
1919

The Mysterious Affair at Styles

Agatha Christie
1920

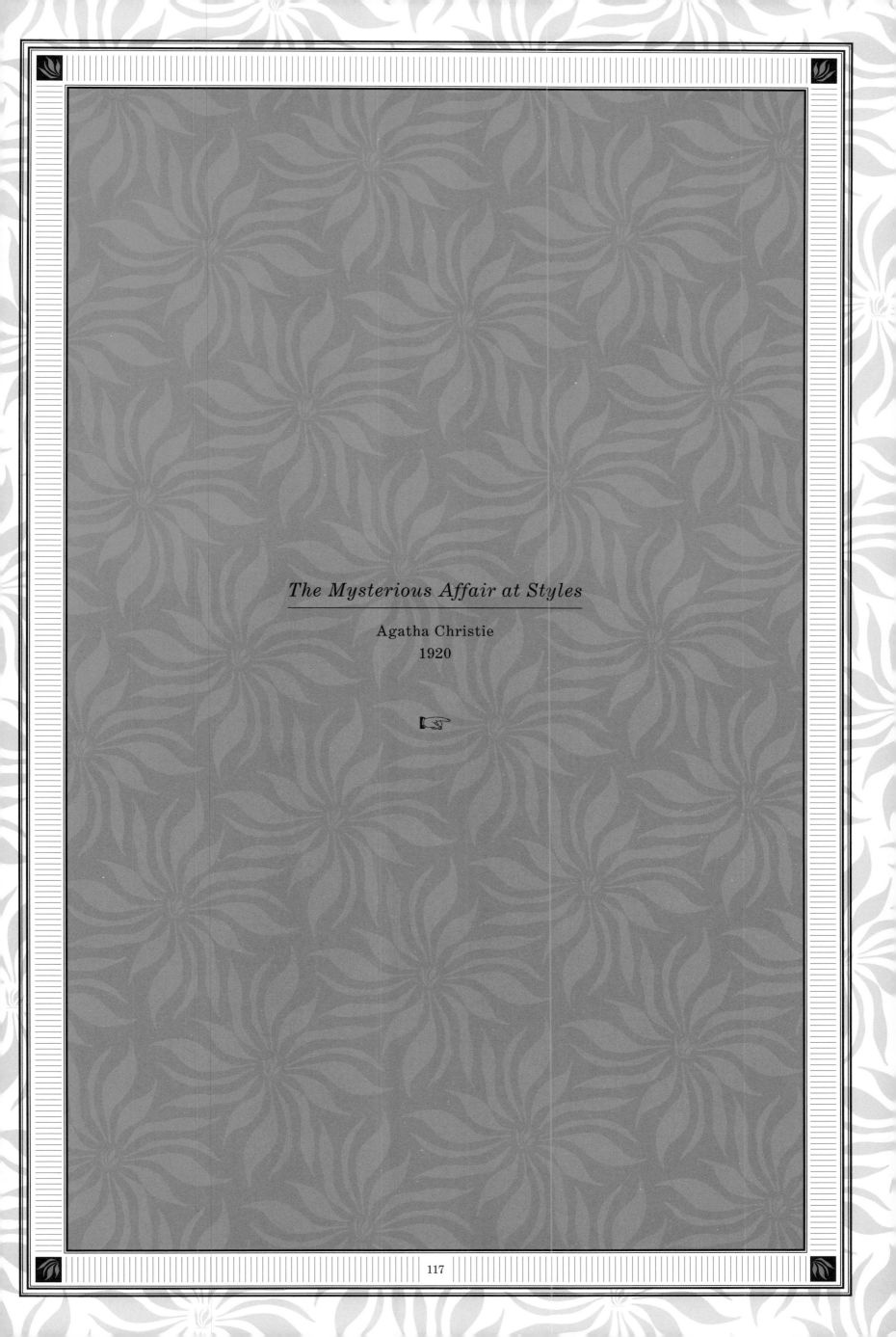

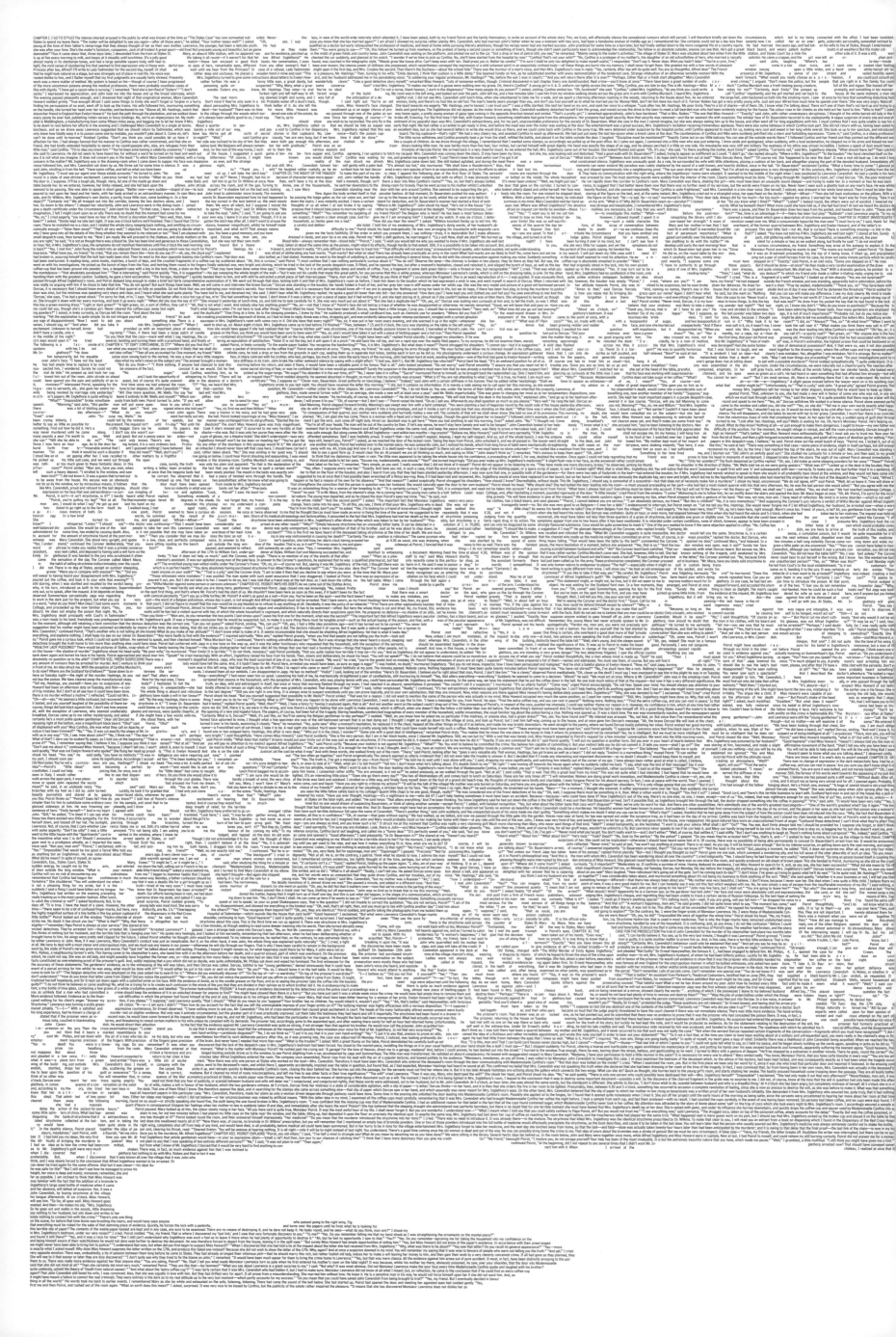

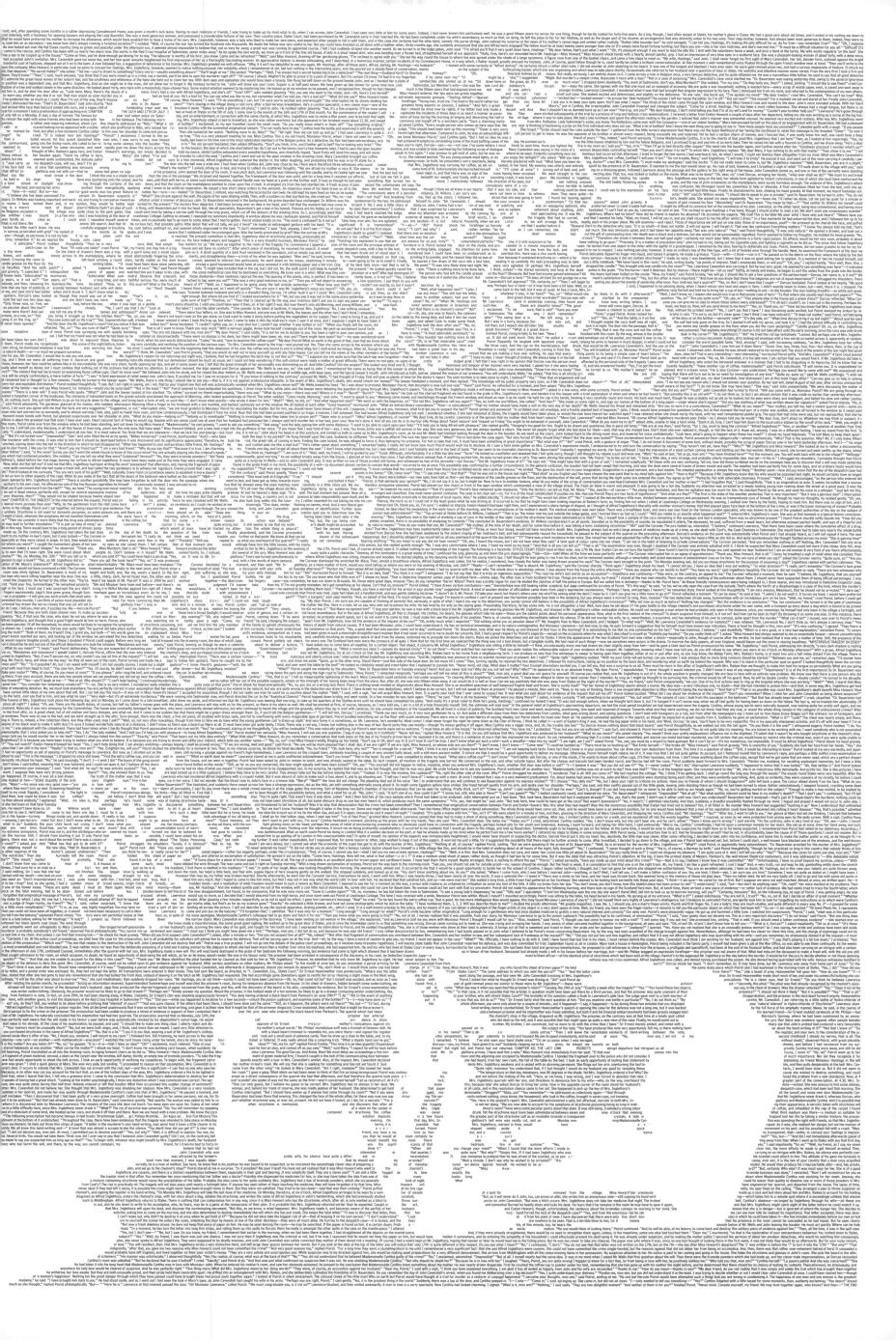

Crome Yellow

Aldous Huxley

1921

Siddhartha

Hermann Hesse

1922

The Curious Case of Benjamin Button

F. Scott Fitzgerald
1922

"The Shunned House"

H. P. Lovecraft
1937

ACKNOWLEDGMENTS

There are many people I need to thank for their help in my personal and professional life. I first want to thank my mom for keeping me grounded— figuratively and literally speaking—my dad for always supporting me, Jim Fan for his always-constructive criticisms, Katherine Collom for tolerating the early days of the business, Michael Kwong for taking Postertext to the next level, Emily Ling for her always amazing illustrations, Jane Gunn for the emotional support and cheerleading, Agne Serpytyte for being my first guinea pig mentee, and the entire Reddit community for being the very first to support Postertext. Without you I would not have been able to start my journey. Final thanks go out to the unique individuals whom I had the pleasure of crossing paths with—some of whom are still traveling to this day. Thank you all, and safe journeys in place and in life.